To Learn by Video for these patterns, please visit
www.go-crafty.com/crochet-in-a-weekend

For pattern inquiries, please visit: www.go-crafty.com

⟩ YARN

1¾oz/50g, 109yd/100m each of
any worsted weight wool blend in
purple (A), mauve (B) and maroon (C)

HOOK

One size H-8 (5mm) crochet hook
OR SIZE TO OBTAIN GAUGE

ADDITIONAL

Stitch marker
Yarn needle

▶ LEARN BY VIDEO
www.go-crafty.com
- Basic stripes
- ch
- Changing colors
- sc
- sl st

⟩ SIZE

Sized for Adult Woman.

⟩ MEASUREMENTS

Head circumference (unstretched)
18"/45.5cm
Length 7½"/19cm

⟩ GAUGE

14 sts and 20 rows to 4"/10cm over sc tbl
using size H-8 (5mm) hook.
TAKE TIME TO CHECK YOUR GAUGE.

⟩ STITCH GLOSSARY

sc tbl single crochet through back loop.
sl st tbl slip stitch through back loop.

⟩ STRIPE PATTERN

[6 rows A, 6 rows B, 6 rows C] 5 times—90
rows in total.

⟩ NOTES

1 Beanie is worked flat, seamed into a tube,
then cinched at the top.
2 When changing colors, work the last sl st
of the row with the new color.

⟩ BEANIE

With A, ch 31.

Foundation row (RS) With A, sl st in 2nd ch
from hook and in next 9 ch, sc in next 15 ch,
sl st in last 5 ch. Ch 1, turn.

Note The foundation row counts as the first
row in the A stripe.

Beg ridge pat

Row 1 (WS) With A, sl st tbl in next 5 sts, sc
tbl in next 15 sts, sl st tbl in last 10 sts. Ch
1, turn.

Row 2 (RS) With A, sl st tbl in next 10 sts,
sc tbl in next 15 sts, sl st tbl in last 5 sts. Ch
1, turn.

Rep rows 1 and 2 for ridge pat, cont in stripe
pat, changing to a new color every 6th row
(at the end of a pat row 1), until all 90 rows
of stripe pat (15 stripes in total) have been
worked, end with a pat row 1. Place last loop
on a stitch marker and do not fasten off.

⟩ FINISHING

Weave in ends. Fold beanie with RS together
with the first A stripe facing you and the last
loop on stitch marker on the right. Insert
hook under 2 loops of starting chain at the
base of row 1, remove stitch marker from
last st and pull this loop through to front,
seam with a sl st working under 2 loops of

the foundation chain on the first row (color
A) and into the back loop only of the stitches
on the last row (color C).

Cinch top

Thread a 1yd/1m length of color B on yarn
needle and double it. Turn beanie with RS
facing out. The top of each slip stitch color
section will look like three vertical rows of
Vs. Insert the yarn needle from right to left
under the center top V of each color section.
You will have 15 "Vs" threaded onto the
doubled yarn. Turn beanie WS out and pull
tightly to cinch top of hat. Tie ends together
and fasten off. ∎

mesh market tote ⟫⟫⟫

YARN

3½oz/100g, 270yd/247m of
any sport weight linen yarn

HOOK

Size D-3 (3.25mm) crochet hook
OR SIZE TO OBTAIN GAUGE

ADDITIONAL

Four small safety pins

> ▶ **LEARN BY VIDEO**
> www.go-crafty.com
> • ch
> • **Crocheting in the round**
> • dc
> • sc
> • sl st

⟩ MEASUREMENTS

Opened Approx 15 x 18"/38 x 45.5cm (excluding handles)
Closed Approx 5½"/14cm diameter

⟩ GAUGE

24 sts and 10 rnds to 4"/10cm over dc using size D-3 (3.25mm) hook.
TAKE TIME TO CHECK YOUR GAUGE.

⟩ TOTE

Pouch/bottom

First circle

Ch 6. Join ch with a sl st forming a ring.
Rnd 1 (RS) Ch 1, work 8 sc in ring, join rnd with a sl st in first sc.
Rnd 2 Ch 2 (counts as 1 dc), work 1 dc in same st as joining, work 2 dc in rem 7 sc, join rnd with a sl st in top of beg ch-2—16 sts.
Rnd 3 Ch 2 (counts as 1 dc), work 1 dc in same place as joining, dc in next st, *work 2 dc in next st, dc in next st; rep from * around, join rnd with a sl st in top of beg ch-2—24 sts.
Rnd 4 Ch 2 (counts as 1 dc), work 1 dc in same place as joining, work 2 dc in each st around, join rnd with a sl st in top of beg ch-2—48 sts.
Rnd 5 Rep rnd 3—72 sts.
Rnd 6 Ch 2 (counts as 1 dc), dc in each st around, join rnd with a sl st in top of beg ch-2.
Rnd 7 Ch 2 (counts as 1 dc), work 1 dc in same place as joining, dc in next 2 sts, *work 2 dc in next st, dc in next 2 sts; rep from * around, join rnd with a sl st in top of beg ch-2—96 sts. Fasten off.

Second circle

Work same as first circle; do *not* fasten off.

Joining

Place second circle on top of first circle with WS tog.
Rnd 8 (RS) Ch 1, working through both layers, sc in next 72 sts, then working in sts of bottom circle only, sc in last 24 sts (this forms the opening of the pouch), join rnd with a sl st in first sc.

Beg mesh sides

Cont to work around second circle *only* as foll:
Rnd 9 (RS) *Ch 6, sk next 2 sts, sc in next st; rep from * around, do not join. Mark last sc worked with a safety pin to indicate end of rnd. You will now be working in a spiral where rnds are not joined.
Rnds 10–24 *Ch 8, sc in next ch-lp of rnd below; rep from * around.
Rnd 25 *Ch 4, sc in next ch-lp of rnd below; rep from * around.

Beg top border

Rnd 26 *Work 4 sc in next ch-lp of rnd below, sc in next sc; rep from * around, join rnd with a sl st in first sc, dropping safety pin.
Rnd 27 Ch 1, sc in each st around, join rnd with a sl st in first sc.

⟩ HANDLES

Mark last st worked with a safety pin (this is marker #1). Divide border into 4 equal sections and mark each point with 3 rem safety pins. Beg with marker #1 and working clockwise, the rem markers are: #2, #3 and #4.
Rnd 28 (first half) Beg at marker #1, work: *2 sc in next st, skip next st; rep from * to marker #3.

First handle

Ch 100, taking care not to twist ch, join ch with 2 sc at marker #2, turn.
Sc in each ch to marker #3, join with 2 sc at marker #3, turn.
Sc in each sc to marker #2, join with 2 sc at marker #2, turn.
Sc in each sc to marker #3, join with 2 sc at marker #3.
Rnd 28 (second half)
Beg at marker #3, work *2 sc in next st, sk next st; rep from * to marker #1.

Second handle

Work same as for first handle between markers #1 and #4. Fasten off.

⟩ FINISHING

To store tote in pouch, turn tote WS out, then turn pouch WS out. Insert tote into pouch. ∎

YARN

14oz/400g, 420yd/748m of any worsted weight silk/wool blend

HOOK

Size K-10½ (6.5mm) crochet hook
OR SIZE TO OBTAIN GAUGE

ADDITIONAL

- 28 stitch markers (optional)
- 2yd/2m matching ³⁄₈"/9mm picot satin ribbon (optional)

▶ **LEARN BY VIDEO**
www.go-crafty.com
- ch
- sc
- tr

⟩ MEASUREMENTS

Width 55¼"/140.5cm
Length 17¾"/45cm

⟩ GAUGE

14 sts and 9 rows to 4"/10cm over lace pat using size K-10½ (6.5mm) crochet hook.
TAKE TIME TO CHECK YOUR GAUGE.

⟩ NOTE

Wrap is worked from the neck down.

⟩ COLLAR

Ch 198. **(Tip** After making foundation chain, use stitch markers to mark stitch repeats for easier counting, beg with 9th chain from hook, then every 7th chain thereafter to end.)
Foundation row Sc in 2nd ch from hook, *ch 7, skip 6 ch, in next ch (or in next ch with stitch marker) work (sc, ch 3, sc, ch 5, sc, ch

3, sc); rep from * to end, ch 7, sc in last ch. (Remove stitch markers.) Turn.
Row 1 *Ch 7, in ch-7 sp work (sc, ch 3, sc, ch 5, sc, ch 3, sc); rep from * to end, ch 3, tr in last sc (becomes ch-7 space for next row). Turn.
Row 2 Ch 1, sc in tr, *ch 7, in ch-7 sp work (sc, ch 3, sc, ch 5, sc, ch 3, sc); rep from *, end last rep with ch 7, sc in last ch-7 sp. Turn.
Rows 3–4 Rep rows 1 and 2.
Row 5 Rep row 1. Fasten off.
Turn work 180 degrees to begin working along opposite foundation row.

⟩ WRAP

Attach yarn to 1st sc at right edge.
Row 1 Rep row 1 of collar.
Row 2 Rep row 2 of collar.
Rows 3–32 Rep rows 1 and 2 for 15 times.
Row 33 Rep row 1.
Turn work 90 degrees to the right to begin side edging.

Side 1 edging

In first ch-sp work (ch 3, sc, ch 5, sc, ch 3, sc), *in next ch-sp work (sc, ch 3, sc, ch 5, sc, ch 3, sc); rep from * 18 times more (last ch-sp is the first ch-sp for collar).
Turn work 90 degrees to the right to begin working along collar.

Collar

*Ch 7, in ch-7 sp work (sc, ch 3, sc, ch 5, sc, ch 3, sc); rep from * to end (last ch-sp is the first sp for side 2 edging).
Turn work 90 degrees to the right to begin side edging.

Side 2 edging

*In next ch-sp work (sc, ch 3, sc, ch 5, sc, ch 3, sc); rep from * 17 times more, in last ch-sp work (sc, ch 3, sc, ch 5, sc, ch 3), sl st in 4th ch of ch-7. Fasten off.

⟩ FINISHING

Gently pull the wrap vertically to align ch st groups. Weave in ends. Block lightly by pinning to finished measurements onto blocking board. With iron, lightly steam without touching wrap. Let dry.

For optional shawl collar

With collar of wrap at top, weave ribbon under and over eyelets under foundation row of collar, beginning and ending 10½"/26.5cm (approx 10th eyelet) from edging. ∎

playful chevron hat ⟫⟫⟫

YARN

Soft by Red Heart, 5oz/141g skeins, each approx 256yd/234m (acrylic) 1 skein each in #9621 true green (A), #9520 seafoam (B), #9518 teal (C), #9870 deep sea (D) and #2515 turquoise (E)

HOOK

One size K-10½ (6.5mm) crochet hook OR SIZE TO OBTAIN GAUGE

> ▶ **LEARN BY VIDEO**
> www.go-crafty.com
> • **Changing colors**
> • **Crocheting in the round**
> • **dc**
> • **dc2tog**
> • **hdc**
> • **Pompom**
> • **tr2tog**
> • **sc**
> • **sc2tog**
> • **sl st**

⟩ SIZE

Sized for Adult Woman.

⟩ MEASUREMENTS

Head circumference 18"/45.5cm
Length 9"/23cm
Note Hat will stretch to fit.

⟩ GAUGE

18 sts and 12 rows to 4"/10cm over chevron pat (rnd 3) using size K-10½ (6.5mm) hook. TAKE TIME TO CHECK YOUR GAUGE.

⟩ STITCH GLOSSARY

tr2tog *Yo twice, insert hook in next st, yo, pull up a loop, [yo, draw through 2 loops] twice*, rep from * to * once, yo and draw through all 3 loops on hook.
dc2tog [Yo, insert hook in next st, yo, pull up a loop, yo, draw through 2 loops] twice, yo and draw through all 3 loops on hook.
sc2tog [Insert hook in next st, yo, pull up a loop] twice, yo and draw through all 3 loops on hook.

⟩ NOTE

Hat is worked in the round from lower edge up, then it is gathered at top. Brim is added afterward.

⟩ HAT

With A, ch 81. Being careful not to twist ch, join with a sl st to first ch.
Rnd 1 (RS) Ch 1, sc in same st as joining and each ch around. Join with sl st to first sc—81 sc.
Rnd 2 Ch 1, sc in same st as joining, sc in next 2 sts, (sc, ch 2, sc) in next st, sc in next 3 sts, *sk next 2 sts, sc in next 3 sts, (sc, ch 2, sc) in next st, sc in next 3 sts; rep from * around to last 2 sts, sk last 2 sts, join with sl st to first sc.
Rnds 3–6 Sl st in next sc, ch 1, sc in same st and next 2 sc, *(sc, ch 2, sc) in next ch-2 sp, sc in next 3 sc, sk 2 sts, sc in next 3 sc; rep from * to last 2 sts, sk last 2 sts, join with sl st to first sc.
Rnds 7–9 With B, sl st in next sc, ch 1, sc in same st and next 2 sc, *(sc, ch 2, sc) in next ch-2 sp, sc in next 3 sc, sk 2 sts, sc in next 3 sc; rep from * to last 2 sts, sk last 2 sts. Join with sl st to first sc.
Rnds 10–12 Rep rnds 7–9 with C.
Rnds 13–15 Rep rnds 7–9 with D.
Rnds 16–18 Rep rnds 7–9 with E.

Rnd 19 With A, sl st in next sc, ch 3 (counts as first dc), hdc in next st, sc in next st, sl st in ch-2 sp, *sc in next st, hdc in next st, dc in next st, tr2tog over next 2 sts, dc in next st, hdc in next st, sc in next st, sl st in ch-2 sp; rep from * to last 5 sts, sc in next st, hdc in next st, dc in next st, tr2tog over last 2 sts, join with sl st to 3rd ch of beg ch-3.
Rnds 20–22 Ch 1, sc in same st as joining and each st around, join with sl st to first sc—72 sc.
Rnd 23 Ch 1, sc in same st as joining and next 5 sts, sc2tog over next 2 sc, *sc in next 6 sts, sc2tog over next 2 sts; rep from * around. Join with sl st to first sc.
Fasten off, leaving a long tail for gathering.

Brim

Rnd 1 Working along other side of foundation ch, join A with a sl st to any point. *Sc in next st, hdc in next 2 sts, dc2tog over next 2 sts, hdc in next 2 sts, sc in next st, sl st in next st; rep from * around, join with sl st to first sl st.
Rnd 2 Ch 1, sc in same st as joining and each st around, join with sl st to first sc—72 sc. Fasten off.

⟩ FINISHING

Weave tail through rnd 23 of hat. Pull tightly to gather. Make a 1½"/4cm pompom with A and attach to top. ▪

festive mobius cowl >>>

YARN

7oz/100g, 198yd/183m of any worsted weight thick and thin cotton blend in variegated blues and greens

HOOKS

Size I/9 (5.5mm) crochet hook
OR SIZE TO OBTAIN GAUGE

ADDITIONAL

Stitch marker

> **LEARN BY VIDEO**
> www.go-crafty.com
> • ch
> • **Crocheting in the round**
> • dc
> • ldc
> • sc
> • sl st

) SIZE

Sized for Medium and Wide and shown in Medium.

) MEASUREMENTS

Circumference 44 (48)"/111.5 (122)cm
Width 14"/35.5cm wide; slightly stretched out as twisted and worn

) GAUGES*

• 12 Fdc or ldc = 4"/10cm using size I/9 (5.5 mm) hook.
• In pat st, 2 st reps = 4"/10cm; 5 row reps = 2¼"/5.5cm using size I/9 (5.5mm) hook.
TAKE TIME TO CHECK YOUR GAUGES.
*Note The yarn used in the sample is thick and thin over long stretches, with the thick sections working slightly larger and the thin sections working slightly smaller. The gauge given here is an average.

) STITCH GLOSSARY

Fdc (foundation double crochet) *This technique creates the sturdy, elastic center line of the mobius construction.*
Begin with a slip knot, ch 4 (equals first "ch" and first "dc"); for the next stitch, yo, insert hook in 4th ch from hook, *yo and draw up a lp (3 loops on hook), yo and draw through one lp on hook for the "ch," [yo and draw through 2 lps on hook] twice for the "dc."*
For the foll sts, yo, insert hook in the ch at the base of the previous st, through the face of the chain and under the nub at the back of the chain (leaving 2 strands at the ch edge), rep from * to * for length of foundation.
Ldc (long double crochet) *This stitch is slightly taller than a dc and also has the benefit of a more balanced appearance front and back, which is nice where both sides of the fabric will be public.*
Yo, insert hook in next st as directed, yo and draw up a lp (3 lps on hook), yo and draw through one lp on hook, [yo and draw through 2 lps on hook] twice.
Spike sc Insert hook under both of next two chain arches (in the big space two rounds below), make sc that encloses both chain arches.

) NOTES

1 Cowl is crocheted in one continuous loop, infinity or mobius style. It begins with a center strip of foundation double crochet, half twisted, with the ends connected to form a figure-8 loop.
2 Lace stitch pattern is worked over a multiple of 6 stitches. To adjust the length of cowl, add or omit multiples of 6 Fdc for the foundation.

) COWL

Foundation rnd Ch 4 (equals first "ch" and first "dc" of Fdc). Place a marker or safety pin in the 4th ch from hook (in other words, in the first ch made). Fdc 131 (143) more, to measure approx 44 (48)"/111.5 (122)cm—132 (144) sts.

Connecting foundation to a mobius rnd

Turn. Bring last dc together with beginning end, give beginning end a half twist, matching last loop on hook with marker in first ch, sl st in first ch. Connect up the row edges of the foundation strip as foll: overlap ends and work 3 sl sts through both layers to connect. Work rnd 1 of pat (see below) across the RS of the 132 (144) "dc" of foundation, make sure to skip the sl st at the place where the strip is connected, then work across the 132 (144) "ch" of foundation. The stitch pattern should line up (mirror image) on either edge of the foundation.
A complete circuit of the mobius figure 8 equals 264 (288) sts, with 44 (48) 6-st reps.
Rnd 1 Ch 1, sc in beg st, sc in next st, [ch 6, skip next 4 sts, sc in each of next 2 sts] 43 (47) times, ch 6, skip rem 4 sts, sl st in beg ch—44 (48) pat reps.
Rnd 2 Ch 3, skip beg sc, dc in next sc, [ch 5, dc in each of next 2 sc] 43 (47) times, ch 5, sl st in 3rd ch of beg ch.
Rnd 3 Ch 3, skip beg dc, dc in next dc, [ch 3, Spike sc in next ch-sp 2 rnds below, ch 3, dc in each of next 2 dc] 43 (47) times, ch 3, Spike sc in last ch-2 sp 2 rnds below, ch 3, sl st in 3rd ch of beg ch.
Rnd 4 Ch 1, sc in beg dc, sc in next dc, [ch 4, sc in each of next 2 dc] 43 (47) times, ch 4, sl st in beg ch.
Rnd 5 Ch 3 (equals ldc), skip beg sc, ldc in next sc, [ldc in each of next 4 chs, ldc in each of next 2 sc] 43 (47) times, ldc in each of last 4 ch, sl st in 3rd ch of beg ch—264 (288) edc.
Rnds 6–15 Rep rnds 1–5 twice, fasten off. Block cowl. ■

simple bucket bag >>>

YARN

10½oz/350g, 686yd/630m of
any worsted weight cotton blend

HOOK

Size E/4 (3.5mm) crochet hook
OR SIZE TO OBTAIN GAUGE

ADDITIONAL

Stitch marker

> **LEARN BY VIDEO**
> www.go-crafty.com
> • ch
> • Crocheting in the round
> • sc
> • sl st

〉 MEASUREMENTS

Circumference 28"/71cm
Length (excluding handles) 12½"/32cm

〉 GAUGE

24 sc and 24 rows to 4"/10cm over sc using
size E/4 (3.5mm) hook.
TAKE TIME TO CHECK YOUR GAUGE.

〉 BAG

Ch 8, join with sl st in first ch to form ring.

Rnd 1 Ch 1, 2 sc in each of next 8 sc, join
with sl st to ch 1—16 sts.

Rnd 2 Ch 1, [1 sc in next sc, 2 sc in next sc]
8 times, join with sl st to ch 1—24 sts.

Rnd 3 Ch 1, sc in each of next 24 sts, join
with sl st to ch 1.

Rnd 4 Ch 1, [1 sc in next 2 sc, 2 sc in next
sc] 8 times, join with sl st to ch 1—32 sts.

Rnd 5 Ch 1, [1 sc in next 3 sc, 2 sc in next
sc] 8 times, join with sl st to ch 1—40 sts.

Rnd 6 Ch 1, [1 sc in next 4 sc, 2 sc in next
sc] 8 times, join with sl st to ch 1—48 sts.

Rnd 7 Ch 1, sc in each of next 48 sts, join
with sl st to ch 1.

Cont to work 1 more sc between inc's until
there are 72 sc, work 1 rnd even, work 3 inc
rnds, work 1 rnd even, work 2 inc rnds—
112 sts.

Work 1 rnd even.

Next rnd Ch 1, [sc in next 13 sc, 2 sc in next
sc] 8 times, join with sl st to ch 1—120 sts.
[Work 1 rnd even, then rep inc rnd, working
1 more sc between inc's] twice—136 sts.
[Work 2 rnds even, then rep inc rnd,
working 1 more sc between inc's] three
times—160 sts.

Next rnd Ch 1, [1 sc in next 19 sc, 2 sc in
next sc] 8 times, join with sl st to ch 1—168
sts. Place marker at end of rnd, do not slip
marker.

Work even in sc for 36 rnds, or until piece
measures 6"/15cm from marker.

Next (handle) rnd Ch 1, sc in next 15 sc, ch
102 sts, skip 54 sc, sc in next 30 sc, ch 102
sts, skip 54 sc, sc in next 15 sc, join with sl st
to ch 1—264 sts.

Next 2 rnds Ch 1, sc in each sc around, join
with sl st to ch 1.

Next rnd Ch 1, sc in next 13 sc, sc2tog, sc in
next sc, sc2tog, sc in next 96 sc, sc2tog, sc in
next sc, sc2tog, sc in next 26 sc, sc2tog, sc in
next sc, sc2tog, sc in next 96 sc, sc2tog, sc in
next sc, sc2tog, sc in next 13 sc, join with sl
st to ch 1—256 sts.

Work 1 rnd even.

Next rnd Ch 1, sc in next 12 sc, sc2tog, sc in
next sc, sc2tog, sc in next 94 sc, sc2tog, sc in
next sc, sc2tog, sc in next 24 sc, sc2tog, sc in
next sc, sc2tog, sc in next 94 sc, sc2tog, sc in
next sc, sc2tog, sc in next 12 sc, join with sl
st to ch 1—248 sts.

Work 1 rnd even.

Next rnd Ch 1, sc in next 11 sc, sc2tog, sc in
next 98 sc, sc2tog, sc in next 22 sc, sc2tog,
sc in next 98 sc, sc2tog, sc in next 11 sc, join
with sl st to ch 1—244 sts.

Work 2 rnds even.

Next rnd Ch 1, sc in next 10 sc, sc2tog, sc in
next 98 sc, sc2tog, sc in next 20 sc, sc2tog, sc
in next 98 sc, sc2tog, sc in next 10 sc—240 sts.

Work 1 rnd even. Fasten off. ■

YARN

Country by Caron International, 3oz/85g skeins, each approx 185yd/170m (microdenier acrylic/merino wool)

- 3 skeins each in #9 renaissance rose (A), #15 deep taupe (C) and #14 deep purple (D)
- 2 skeins in #12 foliage (B)

HOOK

Size G-6 (4mm) crochet hook
OR SIZE TO OBTAIN GAUGE

ADDITIONAL

- Yarn needle
- Fabric glue (optional)

▶ LEARN BY VIDEO
www.go-crafty.com

- ch
- Changing colors
- Crocheting in the round
- sl st
- tr

⟩ MEASUREMENTS

Approx 70"/178cm wide (measured across top edge) x 62"/157.5cm long (measured along each side edge)

⟩ GAUGE

One motif (4 rnds) to 4¾"/12cm in diameter using size G-6 (4 mm) hook.
TAKE TIME TO CHECK YOUR GAUGE.

⟩ TO JOIN MOTIFS

Drop loop from hook, insert hook in (center) dc of neighboring motif(s), pick up dropped loop, draw through, and cont with instructions.

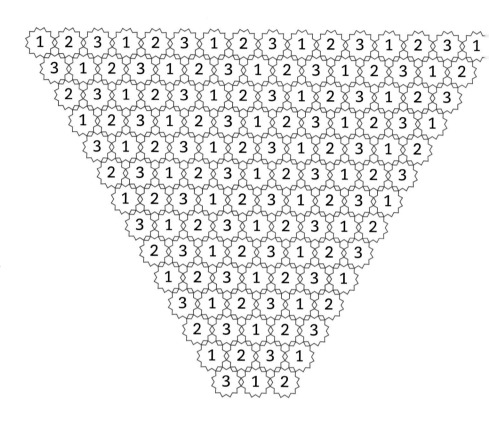

⟩ COLOR SEQUENCE 1

Work rnd 1 with D, rnd 2 with C, rnd 3 with B, rnd 4 with A.

⟩ COLOR SEQUENCE 2

Work rnd 1 with C, rnd 2 with B, rnd 3 with A, rnd 4 with D.

⟩ COLOR SEQUENCE 3

Work rnd 1 with B, rnd 2 with A, rnd 3 with D, rnd 4 with C.

⟩ NOTES

1 Weaving in ends as each motif is completed makes finishing much easier. A dab of fabric glue or fray check applied to cut ends will help prevent ends from working free.

2 To change color in a join, insert hook in beginning ch or first sc, yarn over with new color and draw through all loops on hook. Secure and fasten off old color.

3 Motifs are joined in ch-spaces of Rnd 4. Each motif is joined to neighboring motifs in the center dc of each of two consecutive shells. The assembly diagram shows the arrangement of the motifs, and joining locations.

⟩ MOTIF

(make 133—45 in color sequence 1, 44 in color sequence 2, and 44 in color sequence 3)
Ch 5, join with sl st to first ch to form ring.
Rnd 1 Ch 1, work 12 sc in ring, join with slip st in first sc, changing to next color—12 sc.

arty medallion wrap >>>

Rnd 2 Ch 4 (counts as dc, ch 1), [dc in next sc, ch 1] 11 times, join with slip st in 3rd ch of beginning ch, changing to next color—12 dc, and 12 ch-1 spaces.

Rnd 3 Ch 6 (counts as tr, ch 2), tr in same st as join, ch 1, [(tr, ch 2, tr) in next dc, ch 1] 11 times, join with slip st in 4th ch of beginning ch—24 tr, 12 ch-2 spaces, and 12 ch-1 spaces. Fasten off.

Joining Motifs

Rnd 4 (first motif—unjoined) Join last color with slip st in any ch-2 space, ch 3 (counts as dc), 4 dc in same ch-2 space (beginning shell made), sc in next ch-1 space, *5 dc in next ch-2 space (shell made), sc in next ch-1 space; repeat from * around, join with slip st in top of beginning ch-12 shells. Fasten off.

Note Each motif, following the first motif, is joined to neighboring motifs at the center dc of each of two consecutive shells. Refer to the assembly diagram for arrangement of the Motifs, and joining locations

Rnd 4 (next motifs—joined) Join last color with slip st in any ch-2 space, ch 3 (counts as dc), 2 dc in same ch-2 space; if there is a neighboring motif, work motif-join in corresponding center dc; 2 dc in same ch-2 space, sc in next ch-1 space, *3 dc in next ch-2 space; if there is a neighboring motif, work motif-join in corresponding center dc; 2 dc in same ch-2 space (shell made), sc in next ch-1 space; repeat from * around; join with slip st in top of beginning ch—12 shells. Fasten off.

) FINISHING

Using yarn needle, weave in all ends. Steam lightly (do not press). ■

shell stitch scarf)))

YARN

3½oz/100g, 138yd/126m each in
5 colors (A, B, C, D, E) of any
worsted weight wool yarn

HOOK

Size K-10½ (6.5mm) crochet hook
OR SIZE TO OBTAIN GAUGE

LEARN BY VIDEO
www.go-crafty.com
- ch
- Changing colors
- dc
- sc
- sl st

) MEASUREMENTS

Width 5½"/14cm
Length 67"/170cm (without fringe)

) GAUGE

13 sts and 8 rows to 4"/10cm over shell st
pat using size K-10½ (6.5mm) hook.
TAKE TIME TO CHECK YOUR GAUGE.

) NOTE

When changing colors, work the last 2 loops
of the last stitch of the row with the new
color.

) SHELL STITCH PATTERN

(chain a multiple of 6 plus 2, pat st after the
foundation row is a multiple of 6 sts plus 1)
Foundation row (RS) Sc in 2nd ch from
hook, *skip next 2 ch, work 5 dc in next ch
(whole shell made), skip next 2 ch, sc in
next ch; rep from * to end. Ch 3 (counts as
1 dc), turn.

Rose Callahan

Row 1 Work 2 dc in first st (half shell made),
*skip next 2 dc, sc in next dc, skip next 2 dc,
work 5 dc in next sc; rep from *, end last rep
with 3 dc in last sc (half shell). Ch 1, turn.
Row 2 Sc in first dc, *skip next 2 dc, work 5
dc in next sc, skip next 2 dc, sc in next dc;
rep from *, end last rep with sc in top of t-ch
of row below. Ch 3, turn.
Rep rows 1 and 2 for shell st pat.

) SCARF

With A, ch 218 sts. Work in shell st pat in the
foll stripes: 1 row each A, B, A, C, A, D, E, C,

E, B, E, working ch 1, turn at end of last row
(row 2 of pat).
Last row With E, sc in first sc, *slip stitch in
next 5 dc, sc in next sc; rep from * to end.
Fasten off.

Fringe

Cut strands of each color approx 20"/51cm
long. Using 5 strands for each fringe, attach
fringe to each short end of scarf, matching
the stripe pat. ■

easy striped tote »»»

YARN

Lion Cotton by Lion Brand Yarn,
5oz/142g skeins, each approx
236yd/215m (cotton)

- 2 skeins in #110 navy (A)
- 1 skein in #98 natural (B)

HOOK

One size F/5 (3.75mm) crochet hook
OR SIZE TO OBTAIN GAUGE

ADDITIONAL

Stitch marker

▶ **LEARN BY VIDEO**
www.go-crafty.com

- **Basic stripes**
- **ch**
- **Changing colors**
- **hdc**
- **sc2tog**
- **sl st**

⟩ MEASUREMENTS

Circumference (above base) 30"/76cm
Length 13"/33cm

⟩ GAUGE

14 sts and 13 rnds to 4"/10cm over stripe
pattern using size F/5 (3.75mm) hook.
TAKE TIME TO CHECK YOUR GAUGE.

⟩ STRIPE PATTERN

Rnd 1 With A, ch 2, pm in top of ch, hdc in
each hdc around, join with sl st to marked
ch, remove marker.

Rnd 2 With A, ch 1, pm in top of ch, sc in
each hdc to last hdc, work sc but use new
color for 2nd yo of sc, cont with new color,
join with sl st to marked ch, remove marker.

Rnd 3 With B, rep rnd 1.
Rnd 4 With B, rep rnd 2.
Rep rnds 1–4 for stripe pat.

⟩ NOTE

Bag is worked in joined rnds. Do *not* turn
work.

⟩ BODY

With A, ch 106. Hdc into 3rd ch from hook,
hdc into each ch across—105 sts.
Do *not* turn work. Join with sl st into beg ch.
Ch 1, place marker (pm) into this ch, sc into
each hdc around. Cont in stripe pat, moving
marker to top of ch for each rnd, until rnd 1
of the 3rd B stripe is complete.
Next (dec) rnd With B, ch 1, sc into next
hdc, sc2tog, sc into each of next 50 hdc,
sc2tog, work sc to end of rnd—103 sts.
Cont in stripe pat until rnd 1 of the 5th B
stripe is complete.
Next (dec) rnd With B, ch 1, sc into next
hdc, sc2tog, sc into each of next 49 hdc,
sc2tog, work sc to end of rnd—101 sts.
Cont in stripe pat until rnd 1 of the 7th A
stripe is complete.
Next (dec) rnd With A, ch 1, sc into next
hdc, sc2tog, sc into each of next 48 hdc,
sc2tog, work sc to end of rnd—99 sts.
Cont in stripe pattern until 16 stripes are
complete, being sure to change to A at end
of last rnd.

Top

Rnd 1 Ch 2, pm in top of ch, hdc in each st
around, join with sl st in marked st, remove
marker.
Rnds 2 and 3 Rep rnd 1 twice more.
Rnd 4 (strap openings) Ch 2, 5 hdc into
next 5 hdc, ch 4, skip next 4 hdc, *hdc into
next 10 hdc, ch 5, skip next 5 hdc, hdc into
next 10 hdc, ch 4, skip next 4 hdc*; rep from

* to *, end hdc in next 6 hdc, join with sl st
to beg ch.
Next rnd Ch 2, 5 hdc in next 5 hdc, 4 hdc
into ch-sp, *hdc in next 10 hdc, 5 hdc into
ch-sp, hdc in next 10 hdc, 4 hdc into ch-sp*;
rep from * to *, end hdc in next 6 hdc, join
with sl st to beg ch.
Rep rnd 1 twice. Fasten off.

⟩ BASE

Ch 44.

Inc rnd 1 Hdc into 3rd ch from hook, hdc
into next 41 ch sts, hdc 3 times into next
ch—46 sts.
Place marker in center st of hdc 3. Do *not*
turn. Working into other side of ch, hdc to
last st, hdc 3 times in last st, place marker in
center stitch of hdc 3, join with sl st to beg
of rnd—92 hdc in rnd.
Inc rnd 2 Ch 2, hdc into same st as ch-2,
hdc to 1 st before marked st, hdc 2 times
into next hdc, remove marker, hdc 3 times
into marked st, mark center stitch, hdc 2
times into next st, hdc into each hdc to 1 st
before next marker, hdc 2 times into next
st, remove marker, hdc 3 times into next st,
place marker in center st of hdc 3, join with
sl st to beg ch—8 sts inc'd.
Rep Inc rnd 2 three times more—124 sts.
Fasten off.

⟩ FINISHING

Sew base into lower edge of bag.

Straps

Ch 90. Work 1 hdc into 3rd ch from hook,
work 1 hdc into each ch—89 sts. Turn.
Next row Ch 2, hdc in each hdc across.
Do *not* turn. Working into other side of ch,
work 1 hdc into each ch. Fasten off.
Insert end of strap through one opening at
top of bag. Loop strap around top of bag and

sew end to strap. Rep for other end.
Rep for 2nd strap.

Ties

Make a chain 40"/101.5cm long. Fasten off.
Pull tie ends from front to back through
strap holes, bring ends tog from back to front
through center hole. Make knot around strand
at front (see photo). Rep for other side. ▬

YARN

Eco-Ways by Red Heart, 4oz/113g skeins, each approx 186yd/170m (acrylic/polyester)

• 2 skeins each in #3334 sand (MC) and #3360 mushroom (CC)

HOOK

Size I-9 (5.5mm) crochet hook, OR SIZE TO OBTAIN GAUGE

LEARN BY VIDEO
www.go-crafty.com
• Basic stripes
• ch
• Changing colors
• Crocheting in the round
• dc
• sl st

) MEASUREMENTS

Circumference approx 40½"/103cm
Width 15½"/39.5cm

) GAUGE

16¾ sts and 7½ rows to 4"/10cm over chevron pattern using size I-9 (5.5mm) hook. TAKE TIME TO CHECK YOUR GAUGE.

) CHEVRON PAT

(for gauge swatch only: multiple of 10 sts plus 3)
Ch 23 loosely.
Row 1 Dc in 4th ch from hook and in next 3 ch, *skip next 2 ch, dc in next 4 ch, ch 2, dc in next 4 ch; rep from * to last 6 ch, skip next 2 ch, dc in next 3 ch, 2 dc in last ch. Turn.
Row 2 Ch 3 (counts as 1 dc), dc in first 4 dc, *skip next 2 dc, dc in next 3 dc, (dc, ch 2, dc) in next ch-2 sp, dc in next 3 dc; rep from * to last 5 dc, skip next 2 dc, dc in last 3 dc, 2 dc in beg 3 skipped ch. Turn.
Row 3 Ch 3 (counts as 1 dc), dc in first 4 dc, *skip next 2 dc, dc in next 3 dc, (dc, ch 2, dc) in next ch-2 sp, dc in next 3 dc; rep from * to last 5 dc, skip next 2 dc, dc in last 3 dc, 2 dc in 3rd ch of turning ch-3. Turn.
Rep row 3 for chevron pat in rows.

) NOTES

1 The end of each rnd is worked by joining with sl st to first st, then turning to work next rnd.
2 When changing colors for new rnd, use the new color to work the sl st when joining at the end of the rnd.
3 When adding yarn in the middle of the rnd, work st leaving the last 2 lps on the hook, then with new yarn, complete the st.

) COWL

With MC, ch 170 loosely. Without twisting foundation ch, join with sl st to back of 1st ch.
Rnd 1 Ch 3 (counts as 1 dc), working in back of foundation ch, dc in next ch, *skip 2 ch, dc in next 4 ch, ch 2, dc in next 4 ch; rep from * around, end last rep with skip 2 ch, dc in next 4 ch, ch 2, dc in last 2 ch. Join with sl st to 3rd ch of beg ch-3. Turn.
Rnd 2 Ch 3 (counts as dc), dc in next 2 sts, *(dc, ch 2, dc) in ch-2 sp, dc in next 3 sts, skip 2 ch, dc in next 3 sts; rep from * around, end last rep with (dc, ch 2, dc) in ch-2 sp, dc in next 3 sts, skip 2 ch. Join with sl st to 3rd ch of beg ch-3. Turn.
Rnd 3 Sl st in 1st and 2nd sts, ch 3 (counts as 1 dc), dc in next 2 sts, *(dc, ch 2, dc) in ch-2 sp, dc in next 3 sts, skip 2 ch, dc in next 3 sts; rep from * around, end last rep with (dc, ch 2, dc) in ch-2 sp, dc in next 3 sts, skip 2 ch. Join with sl st to 3rd ch of beg ch-3. Turn.

Rep rnd 3 for chevron pat in the round and work in the foll stripe pat: 2 rnds MC, 2 rnds CC, 1 rnd MC, 5 rnds CC, 2 rnds MC, 1 rnd CC, 5 rnds MC, 2 rnds CC, 1 rnd MC, 5 rnds CC. Fasten off. ■

shell-pattern armwarmers »»

YARN

5¼oz/150g balls, 347yd/400m
of any sport weight, variegated,
wool/nylon blend yarn

HOOK

Size F-5 (3.75mm) hook
OR SIZE TO OBTAIN GAUGE

▶ LEARN BY VIDEO
www.go-crafty.com
- chain
- dc
- sc
- sl st

❭ MEASUREMENTS

Circumference 7"/18cm
Length (including edging) 8½"/21.5cm

❭ SIZE

Sized for Adult Woman.

❭ GAUGE

3 st reps (sc and 5-dc shell = 1 rep) and 11
rows to 4"/10cm over shell st using size F-5
(3.75mm) hook.
TAKE TIME TO CHECK YOUR GAUGE.

❭ SHELL STITCH

(chain a multiple of 6 sts plus 2)
Row 1 Sc in 2nd ch from hook, *skip 2 ch, 5
dc in next ch (shell st), skip 2 ch, sc in next
ch; rep from * to end. Ch 3, turn.
Row 2 Work 2 dc in first sc, skip 2 dc, sc in
next dc (center of 5-dc shell from previous
row), *5 dc in next sc, skip 2 dc, sc in next dc;
rep from *, end 3 dc in last sc. Ch 1, turn.

Row 3 Work sc in first dc, *5 dc in next
sc, skip 2 dc, sc in next dc (center of 5-dc
shell from previous row); rep from * to end,
working last sc in top of t-ch. Ch 3, turn.
Rep rows 2 and 3 for shell st.

❭ LEFT ARMWARMER

Ch 38. Work rows 1–3 of shell st, then rep
rows 2 and 3 eight times. Do *not* fasten off.

❭ FINISHING

Turn work and fold foundation up to last
row just worked. Join foundation row to last
row with sl st, working in shell pat row 2
along working row, as foll:
Joining row (RS) Sl st into sc on foundation
row, 2 dc in 1st sc, skip 2 dc, sc in next dc, sl
st in base of 5-dc shell on foundation ch, 5
dc in next sc, skip 2 dc, sc in next dc, leave
corresponding sc and 5-dc shell on foundation ch unworked (thumb opening made), [3
dc in next sc, sl st in base of corresponding
sc on foundation ch, 2 dc in same sc, skip 2
dc, sc in next dc, sl st in base of 5-dc shell on
foundation ch] 4 times, 3 dc in next sc, sl st
in base of sc on foundation ch.
Fasten off.

Edging

With RS facing, join yarn and work sc in one
corner at top of armwarmer. Working across
top opening, alternate 5-dc shell and sc
evenly spaced so that there are 6 shells, join
rnd with sl st in 1st sc.
Fasten off.

❭ RIGHT ARMWARMER

Work as for left armwarmer to joining row.
Joining row (RS) Sl st into sc on foundation
row, 2 dc in first sc, [skip 2 dc, sc in next dc,
sl st in base of 5-dc shell on foundation ch,

3 dc in next sc, sl st in base of corresponding
sc on foundation ch, 2 dc in same sc] 4 times,
skip 2 dc, sc in next dc, leave corresponding
sc and 5-dc shell on foundation ch unworked
(thumb opening made), 5 dc in next sc, skip 2
dc, sc in next dc, sl st in base of 5-dc shell on
foundation ch, 3 dc in next sc, sl st in base of
sc on foundation ch.
Fasten off.
Work edging as for left armwarmer. ▪

cozy chain stitch cowl ⟩⟩⟩

YARN
3½oz/100g, 147yd/134m of any bulky wool/alpaca/silk blend

HOOK
One size J-10 (6mm) crochet hook OR SIZE TO OBTAIN GAUGE

ADDITIONAL
Stitch marker

▶ LEARN BY VIDEO
www.go-crafty.com
- ch
- Crocheting in the round
- dc
- sc
- sl st

⟩ MEASUREMENTS
Circumference 21"/53.5cm
Length 12"/30.5cm

⟩ GAUGE
16 chain sts to 4"/10cm using size J-10 (6mm) hook.
TAKE TIME TO CHECK YOUR GAUGE.

⟩ COWL
Ch 84. Join with sl st to form ring. Place marker to mark end of rnd and move marker up as rnds are worked.

Rnd 1 *Ch 5, skip next 5 ch, sc in next ch; rep from * around, end with sc in marked sl st—14 ch-5 lps.

Rnd 2 *Ch 5, skip next ch-5 lp, sc in next sc; rep from * around—14 ch-5 lps.

Rnd 3 *Ch 7, skip next ch-5 lp, sc in next sc; rep from * around—14 ch-7 lps.

Rnd 4 *Ch 7, skip ch-7 lp, sc in next sc, rep from * around—14 ch-7 lps.

Rnd 5 Ch 2, *sc into space 2 rnds below next ch-7 lp, ch 5; rep from * around, end with ch 2, dc in last sc—13 ch-5 lps.

Rnd 6 Ch 2, skip next ch-2 space, sc in next sc, *ch 5, skip next ch-5 lp, sc in next sc; rep from * around, end with ch 2, sc in dc—13 ch-5 lps.

Rnd 7 Ch 3, skip next ch-2 space, sc in next sc, *ch 7, skip next ch-5 lp, sc in next sc; rep from * around, end with ch 3, skip next ch-2 space, dc in last sc—13 ch-7 lps.

Rnd 8 Ch 3, skip next ch-3 lp, sc in next sc, *ch 7, skip next ch-7 lp, sc in next sc; rep from * around, end with ch 3, skip next ch-3 lp, sc in last sc—13 ch-7 lps.

Rnd 9 Ch 5, skip next ch-3 lp and sc into next sc, sc into space 2 rnds below next ch-7 lp, *ch 5, sc into space 2 rnds below next ch-7 lp; rep from * around, end with sc in last sc—14 ch-5 lps.

Rep rnds 2–9 three times more. Then rep rnd 2 twice. Fasten off. ▮

easy v-stitch wristers 〉〉〉

YARN

3½oz/100g hanks, 425yd/389m
of any fingering weight wool/nylon
blend

HOOK

Size D-3 (3.25mm) hook
OR SIZE TO OBTAIN GAUGE

> ▶ **LEARN BY VIDEO**
> www.go-crafty.com
> • ch
> • dc
> • sc

〉 SIZE

Sized for Adult Woman.

〉 MEASUREMENTS

Wrist circumference 7"/18cm
Hand circumference (at widest part of
thumb gusset) 10"/25.5cm
Length 6½"/16.5cm

〉 GAUGE

8 V-sts and 16 rows to 4"/10cm over V-st pat
using size D-3 (3.25mm) hook.
TAKE TIME TO CHECK YOUR GAUGE.

〉 V-STITCH PATTERN

(chain a multiple of 3)
V-st Work (dc, ch 1, dc) in one sc.
Row 1 (RS) Sc in 2nd ch from hook and in
each ch to end. Ch 3, turn.
Row 2 *Skip 2 sc, V-st in next sc; rep from *
to last 2 sts, skip 1 sc, dc in last sc. Ch 1, turn.
Row 3 Sc in each dc and ch-1 sp across, end
sc in top of t-ch. Ch 3, turn.
Rep rows 2 and 3 for V-st pat.

〉 CUFF

Ch 42.
Row 1 (RS) Sc in 2nd ch from hook and in
each ch to end—41 sc. Ch 3, turn.
Beg with row 2, work in V-st pat (13 V-sts on
row 2 and 41 sc on row 3) until there are 9
rows from beg, end with a pat row 3.

Thumb gusset

Row 10 (inc—WS) [Skip 2 sc, V-st in next
sc] 6 times, skip 2 sc, (dc, ch 1, dc, ch 1, dc)
in next sc (1 V-st inc for thumb), cont in pat
to end.
Row 11 Work pat row 3—43 sc.
Row 12 [Skip 2 sc, V-st in next sc] 7 times,
skip 1 sc, V-st in next sc, *skip 2 sc, V-st in
next sc; rep from *, end skip 1 sc, dc in last
sc—14 V-sts.
Row 13 Work pat row 3—44 sc.
Row 14 (inc) [Skip 2 sc, V-st in next sc] 6
times, [skip 2 sc, inc 1 V-st in next sc] twice,
cont in pat to end.
Row 15 Work pat row 3—48 sc.
Row 16 [Skip 2 sc, V-st in next sc] 6 times,
skip 1 sc, V-st in next sc, skip 2 sc, V-st in
next dc, skip 1 sc, V-st in next sc, *skip 2 sc,
V-st in next sc; rep from *, end skip 1 sc, dc
in last sc—16 V-sts.
Row 17 Work pat row 3—50 sc.
Row 18 (inc) [Skip 2 sc, V-st in next sc] 6
times, skip 2 sc, inc 1 V-st in next sc, [skip 2
sc, V-st in next sc] twice, skip 2 sc, inc 1 V-st
in next sc, *skip 2 sc, V-st in next sc; rep from
*, end skip 1 sc, dc in last sc.
Row 19 Work pat row 3—54 sc.
Row 20 [Skip 2 sc, V-st in next sc] 7 times,
skip 1 sc, V-st in next sc, [skip 2 sc, V-st in
next dc] 3 times, skip 1 sc, V-st in next sc,
*skip 2 sc, V-st in next sc; rep from *, end
skip 1 sc, dc in last sc—18 V-sts.
Row 21 Work pat row 3—56 sc.
Work 2 rows even in pat.

Thumb opening

Next row [Skip 2 sc, V-st in next sc] 6 times,
ch 3, skip 20 sc, V-st in next sc, *skip 2 sc,
V-st in next sc; rep from *, end skip 1 sc, dc
in last sc.
Next row Sc in each dc and ch-1 sp across, 3
sc in ch-3 sp—41 sc.
Work 4 rows even in pat.
Fasten off.

〉 FINISHING

Fold wristlet in half lengthwise with WS tog.
Sc the long side tog so that the sc ridge will
show on the RS. ∎

toasty triangle shawl ⟫⟫⟫

YARN

Heartland Thick & Quick by Lion Brand Yarn, 5oz/142g skeins, each approx 125yd/114m (acrylic)
- 3 skeins in #098 acadia (A)
- 1 skein each in #135 yosemite (B) and #151 katmai (C)

HOOK

One size P/Q (15mm) crochet hook OR SIZE TO OBTAIN GAUGE

LEARN BY VIDEO
www.go-crafty.com

- ch
- dc
- dc2tog
- hdc
- sc
- sl st

⟩ MEASUREMENTS

Width 64"/162.5cm
Depth 32"/81cm

⟩ GAUGE

13 sts = 6"/15 cm and 11 rows = 8"/20.5 cm over dc/sl st pat st using size P/Q (15mm) crochet hook.
TAKE TIME TO CHECK YOUR GAUGE.

⟩ STITCH GLOSSARY

Dc2tog [Yo hook and draw up a loop in next st, yo through 2 loops on hook] twice, yo and through all 3 loops—1 st dec'd.

⟩ NOTE

The dc/sl st pat st is worked using A (or C) for the dc rows and B for all the sl st rows. Work the sl st rows loosely and drop yarn just worked at the end of the row to be picked up and worked from that side as described.

⟩ SHAWL

Beg at outside edge with A, ch 152.
Row 1 (RS) With A, work 1 dc in 3rd ch from hook, [dc2tog] twice, 1 dc in each of next 67 ch, dc2tog, skip 2 ch, dc2tog, work 1 dc in each of next 67 ch, [dc2tog] twice, 1 dc in last ch, drop A.
Row 2 (WS) With B, ch 1, then working into front loops only, working loosely, work 1 sl st in each st to end, drop B.
Row 3 (WS) Return to the WS and with dropped A, ch 2 (does not count as 1 dc on this or any row), working into both loops, work 1 dc, [dc2tog] twice, then work dc to 3 dc before the center dc (or 63 dc), dc2tog, and skip the center 2 sts, then dc2tog, work 63 dc, [dc2tog] twice, work 1 dc, drop A and turn.
Row 4 (RS) From beg of the RS row and with B, ch 1, work 1 sl st in back loop only of each st to end, drop B.
Row 5 (WS) Join C, ch 2, working into front loops only, work 1 dc, [dc2tog] twice, work 59 dc (or to 3 sts before the center), dc2tog, skip center 2 sts, dc2tog, work 59 dc, [dc2tog] twice, work 1 dc, cut C.
Row 6 (WS) With dropped B, ch 1, sl st in front loop of each st, drop B
Row 7 (RS) With A, ch 2, working in both loops, work 1 dc, [dc2tog] twice, work 55 dc (or 3 sts before the center), dc2tog, skip center 2 sts, dc2tog, work 55 dc, [dc2tog] twice, work 1 dc, drop A.
Row 8 (RS) With B, ch 1, sl st through back loops only. Drop B.
Row 9 (WS) With A, ch 2, working into front loops only, work 1 dc, [dc2tog] twice, work 51 dc (or 3 sts before the center), dc2tog, skip center 2 sts, dc2tog, work 51 dc, [dc2tog] twice, work 1 dc, cut A.

Row 10 (WS) With dropped B, rep row 2.
Row 11 (WS) With A, rep row 3 only with 47 (not 63) dc.
Row 12 (RS) With B, rep row 4.
Row 13 (WS) With C, rep row 5 only with 43 (not 59) dc.
Row 14 (WS) With B, rep row 6.
Row 15 (RS) With A, rep row 7 only with 39 (not 55) dc.
Row 16 (RS) With B, rep row 8.
Row 17 (WS) With A, rep row 9 only with 35 (not 51) dc. Cut A.
Row 18 (WS) With B, rep row 2.
Row 19 (WS) With A, rep row 3 only with 31 (not 63) dc.
Row 20 (RS) With B, rep row 4.
Row 21 (WS) With C, rep row 5 only with 27 (not 59) dc.
Row 22 (WS) With B, rep row 6.
Row 23 (RS) With A, rep row 7 only with 23 (not 55) dc.
Row 24 (RS) With B, rep row 8.
Row 25 (WS) With A, rep row 9 only with 19 (not 51) dc. Cut A.
Row 26 (WS) With B, rep row 2.
Row 27 (WS) With A, rep row 3 only with 15 (not 63) dc.
Row 28 (RS) With B, rep row 4.
Row 29 (WS) With C, rep row 5 only with 11 (not 59) dc.
Row 30 (WS) With B, rep row 6.
Row 31 (RS) With A, rep row 7 only with 7 (not 55) dc.
Row 32 (RS) With B, rep row 8.
Row 33 (WS) With A, rep row 9 only with 3 (not 51) dc.
Row 34 (WS) With B, rep row 2–14 sl sts.
Row 35 (RS) With A, working in both loops, ch 2, work 2 dc, 2 hdc, 2 sc, skip 2 sts, work 2 sc, 2 hdc, 2 dc. Cut yarn and fold at center of the V, and seam the center tog.

〉FINISHING
Upper edge trim
Row 1 From the WS with A, ch 1 and work 114 sc along the upper edge, turn.
Row 2 (WS) Ch 2, 2 hdc in first st, hdc in each st to last st, 2 hdc in last st. Fasten off. Sew in ends. ▨

Jack Deutsch

cute striped hat >>>

YARN

- 1¾oz/50g, 122yd/112m of any worsted weight wool (A)
- 1¾oz/50g, 106yd/97m of any worsted weight mohair blend (B)

HOOK

One each sizes G-6 and H-8 (4 and 5mm) crochet hooks OR SIZE TO OBTAIN GAUGE

▶ LEARN BY VIDEO
www.go-crafty.com
- ch
- Crocheting in the round
- dc
- hdc
- sc
- sl st

⟩ SIZE

Sized for Adult Woman.

⟩ MEASUREMENTS

Brim circumference 20"/51cm
Length 7½"/19cm

⟩ GAUGE

16 dc and 4 dc rnds to 4"/10 cm over pat st using larger hook.
TAKE TIME TO CHECK YOUR GAUGE.

⟩ NOTE

When joining a new color, join with sl st before beg the rnd.

⟩ HAT

With larger hook and A, leaving a long tail, ch 4, join with sl st in first ch to form ring.
Rnd 1 With A, ch 1, work 8 sc in ring, join with sl st in first sc.
Rnd 2 With A, ch 1, work 2 sc in each sc around—16 sc. Join with sl st to first st on this and all foll rnds.
Rnd 3 With A, ch 3, skip first sc, [hdc in next sc, ch 1] 15 times, end join with sl st to 2nd ch of ch-3.
Rnd 4 With B, ch 2, then working back into the sc on rnd 2 (and working over the ch-1 space of previous rnd), *work 1 dc in the rnd 2 sc, ch 1; rep from * 15 times more.
Rnd 5 With A, ch 1, work 1 sc in each dc and 1 sc in each ch-1 space—32 sc. Join.
Rnd 6 With A, ch 1, [work 1 sc, ch 1] 32 times, join to first sc.
Rnd 7 With B, ch 2, [work 1 sc in ch-1 space, ch 1] 32 times, join to 2nd ch of the ch-2.
Rnd 8 With A, rep rnd 7.
Rnd 9 With A, ch 3 (does not count as 1 dc), working into back loops only of each sc or into the chain (not the ch-space), [work 4 dc, 2 dc in next st] 12 times, work 4 dc—76 dc, join to top of ch-3.
Rnd 10 With B, ch 4, [skip 1 st, working into back loop, dc in next st, ch 1] 38 times, join to 3rd ch of the ch-4. There are 39 ch-spaces.
Rnd 11 With A, ch 1, work 1 sc in top of ch-3, *1 sc into the ch (not the ch-space), 1 sc in back loop of the dc; rep from * around, join to first sc—78 sc.
Rnd 12 With A, ch 3, working into back loops, work 1 dc in each st around, join to top of ch-3.
Rnd 13 With B, ch 1, sc in first st, *ch 1, skip 1 st, sc in next st; rep from *, end ch 1, join to first sc.

Rnd 14 With A, ch 2, *sc in next ch-space, ch 1; rep from *, end sc in last space, join in the ch-2 space—39 sc and ch-1 spaces.
Rnd 15 With A, ch 3, *[1 dc in the chain (not the ch-space), 1 dc in back loop of the dc] 4 times, 2 dc in the next chain, [1 dc in the back loop of the dc, 1 dc in the chain] 4 times, 2 dc in the back loop of the dc; rep from * 3 times more, end [1 dc in the chain, 1 dc in the back loop of the dc] 3 times—86 dc.
Rnd 16 With B, ch 4, *skip next dc, 1 dc in back loop of next dc, ch 1; rep from *, end sl st in 3rd ch of ch-4.
Rnd 17 With A, ch 1, work 1 sc in each ch and 1 sc in back loop of each dc, join. Change to smaller hook.
Rnd 18 With A, ch 3, working in back loops only, work 1 dc in each st around, join.
Rnd 19 Rep rnd 18.
Rnd 20 With B, ch 1, work 1 sc in back loop of first st, *ch 1, skip 1 st, sc in back loop of next st; rep from *, end ch 1, sl st in first sc.
Rnd 21 With A, ch 2, sc in first ch-1 space, *ch 1, sc in next ch-1 space; rep from *, end join with sl st in ch-2.
Rnd 22 With B, ch 1, work 1 sc in back loop of each sc and 1 sc in each ch (not the ch-space) around. Join and fasten off.

⟩ FINISHING

Return to top of hat. With smaller hook, ch 8 with the tail of A, join to opposite side of ring to form a loop. Work 1 sc in each chain and fasten off. Block lightly to measurements. ■

quick mesh wristers 》》》

YARN

1¾oz/50g hanks, 175yd/160m
of any wool sock yarn

HOOK

Size E-4 (3.5mm) hook
OR SIZE TO OBTAIN GAUGE

LEARN BY VIDEO
www.go-crafty.com
- ch
- Crocheting in the round
- sc
- sl st

》 SIZE

Sized for Adult Woman.

》 MEASUREMENTS

Wrist circumference 6"/15cm
Hand circumference 7"/18cm
Length 6½"/16.5cm

》 GAUGE

24 sc and 24 rows to 4"/10cm over sc rib
using size E-4 (3.5mm) hook.
TAKE TIME TO CHECK YOUR GAUGE.

》 SC RIB

(over any number of ch)
Row 1 Sc in 2nd ch from hook and in each
ch to end. Ch 1, turn.
Row 2 Working into back loop only, work sc
in each sc. Ch 1, turn.
Rep row 2 for sc rib.

》 WRISTERS

Cuff

Ch 11.
Row 1 Sc in 2nd ch from hook and in each
ch across. Ch 1, turn—10 sc.
Cont in sc rib until piece measures 6"/15cm
from beg, and on last row, ch 1, turn and
work along the long edge as foll:

Hand

Next row (RS) Work 40 sc across long edge
of cuff.
Join to work in rnds and cont in mesh pat
as foll:
Rnd 1 Ch 1, join with sc in first sc of row
just worked, *ch 5, skip 3 sc, sc in next sc; rep
from * around, end ch 5, sl st in first sc—10
ch-5 sps.
Rnd 2 Ch 5, sc in first ch-5 sp, *ch 5, sc in
next ch-5 sp; rep from * around, end ch 2, sc
in 3rd ch of beg ch-5—9 ch-5 sps.
Rnd 3 *Ch 5, sc in next ch-5 sp; rep from *
around, end ch 5, sl st in first sc.
Rnds 4–11 Rep rnds 2 and 3 four times.

Thumb opening

Rnd 12 Ch 5, sc in first ch-5 sp, [ch 5, sc in
next ch-5 sp] 3 times, ch 5, skip 2 ch-5 sps
(for thumb opening), sc in next ch-5 sp, *ch
5, sc in next ch-5 sp; rep from * around, end
ch 2, sc in 3rd ch of beg ch-5—8 ch-5 sps.
Rnd 13 Rep rnd 3.
Rnd 14 Rep rnd 2.
Rnd 15 Sc evenly spaced around, working 2
sc in each ch-2 sp, 5 sc in each ch-5 sp and
skip each sc.
Join rnd with sl st to first sc.
Rnd 16 Ch 1, sc in each sc around.
Join rnd with sl st to first sc.
Fasten off.

》 FINISHING

Sew cuff seam. ▓

cool cuffed hat >>>

YARN

3½oz/100g, 220yd/200m of worsted weight wool yarn each in ecru/tan tweed (A) and red (B)

HOOK

One each sizes I-9 and J-10 (5.5 and 6mm) hooks
OR SIZE TO OBTAIN GAUGE

LEARN BY VIDEO
www.go-crafty.com

- ch
- Changing colors
- Crocheting in the round
- hdc
- sl st

) SIZE

Sized for Adult Woman.

) MEASUREMENTS

Circumference 20"/51cm
Depth 8"/20.5cm

) GAUGE

13 hdc and 10 rnds to 4"/10 cm over hdc pat st using larger hook.
TAKE TIME TO CHECK YOUR GAUGE.

) HAT

With larger hook and A, ch 4, join with a sl st to first ch to form ring.

Rnd 1 Ch 2 (does not count as 1 hdc), work 8 hdc in ring, join to top of ch-2 on this and all foll rnds.

Rnd 2 Ch 2, work 2 hdc in each hdc around, join on this and all foll rnds—16 hdc.

Rnd 3 Ch 2, *work 1 hdc, 2 hdc in next hdc; rep from * around—24 hdc.

Rnd 4 Ch 2, *2 hdc in next hdc, work 3 hdc; rep from * around—30 hdc.

Rnd 5 Ch 2 [work 3 hdc, 2 hdc in next hdc] 7 times, work 2 hdc—37 hdc.

Rnd 6 Ch 2, [work 4 hdc, 2 hdc in next hdc] 7 times, work 2 hdc—44 hdc.

Rnd 7 Ch 2, [work 5 hdc, 2 hdc in next hdc] 7 times, work 2 hdc—51 hdc.

Rnd 8 Ch 2, [work 6 hdc, 2 hdc in next hdc] 7 times, work 2 hdc—58 hdc.

Rnd 9 Ch 2, [work 7 hdc, 2 hdc in next hdc] 7 times, work 2 hdc—65 hdc.

Rnd 10 Ch 2, work even in hdc around.

Rnds 11–21 Rep rnd 10.

Change to smaller hook and turn to work the brim rnds from the WS (for turn back).

Rnd 22 (WS) Working in back loops only, ch 2, work in hdc around.

Rnd 23 (WS) Rep rnd 10.

Rnd 24 With B, ch 1, then working in back loops only, work 1 sc in each st around.

Rnd 25 With B, ch 1, working through both loops, work 1 sc in each st around.

Rnds 26–28 With A, rep rnd 10. Cut A.

Rnd 29 With B, ch 1, working through back loops only, work 1 sl st in each st around.
Join and fasten off. ∎

bobble-edge purse ⟩⟩⟩

YARN

- 7oz/200g, 310yd/284m of any worsted weight wool in bright green (A)
- 3½oz/100g skeins, 155yd/142m in lime green (B)

HOOK

Size I-9 (5.5mm) crochet hook
OR SIZE TO OBTAIN GAUGE

ADDITIONAL

Stitch markers

LEARN BY VIDEO
www.go-crafty.com
- ch
- hdc
- hdc2tog
- Popcorn
- sc2tog

⟩ MEASUREMENTS

Width approx 14"/35.5cm
Length approx 9"/23cm (with popcorn edging)

⟩ GAUGE

15 sts and 9 rows to 4"/10cm over hdc (working into back lps) using size I-9 (5.5mm) crochet hook.
TAKE TIME TO CHECK YOUR GAUGE.

⟩ STITCH GLOSSARY

hdc2tog [Yo and draw up a lp in next st] twice, yo and draw through all 5 lps on hook—1 st decreased.

sc2tog [Draw up a lp in next st] twice, yo and draw through all 3 lps on hook—1 st decreased.

Popcorn [Yo and draw up a lp, yo and draw through 2 lps on hook] 4 times, yo and draw through all 5 lps on hook—popcorn made.

⟩ BAG

With A, ch 18.
Row 1 Hdc in 3rd st from hook, hdc in next 3 ch, 2 hdc in next ch, hdc in next 5 ch, 2 hdc in next ch, hdc in last 5 ch, turn—19 sts.
Row 2 Ch 2 (counts as 1 hdc at beg of this and every foll row), working into back lps, hdc in next 5 sts, 2 hdc in next st, hdc in next 5 sts, 2 hdc in next st, hdc in last 6 sts, turn—21 sts.
Note Cont to work into back lp of each hdc unless otherwise stated.
Row 3 Ch 2, hdc in next 6 sts, 2 hdc in next st (inc made), place a marker in 2nd st of inc, hdc in next 5 sts, 2 hdc in next st (inc made), place a marker in first st of inc, hdc in last 7 sts, turn—23 sts.
Move markers up to corresponding st in next row as work progresses.
Rows 4–14 Ch 2, hdc in each st across to marked st, 2 hdc in next st marked st, hdc in next 5 sts, 2 hdc in next marked st, hdc in each rem st to end, turn—45 sts at end of row 14.
Rows 15–38 Ch 2, hdc in each st to end, turn.
Row 39 Ch 2, hdc in next 17 sts, hdc2tog in next 2 sts, hdc in next 5 sts, hdc2tog in next 2 sts, hdc in last 18 sts, turn—43 sts.
Place a marker in each hdc2tog, move markers up to corresponding dec st in each row as work progresses.
Rows 40–51 Ch 2, hdc across to 1 st before marker, hdc2tog in next 2 sts, hdc in next 5 sts, hdc2tog in next 2 sts, hdc in each st to end, turn—19 sts at end of row 51.
Row 52 Ch 2, hdc in next 4 sts, hdc2tog in next 2 sts, hdc in next 5 sts, hdc2tog in next 2 sts, hdc in last 5 sts—17 sts. Do *not* fasten off.

Popcorn edging

Work along side edge from row 52 to row 1 as foll:
Row 53 Work 27 hdc to end. Turn.
Work side edge as foll: .
Row 54 *Sc in next 5 sts, sc2tog over next 2 sts; rep from * twice more, sc to end—24 sts. Cut A, join B.
Row 55 With B, ch 1, sc 1, *popcorn in next st, sc in next st; rep from * to end, sc2tog—11 popcorns.
Row 56 With B, sc in each st. Fasten off.
Reattach A to other side edge and work rows 53–56 in the same manner.

⟩ STRAP

With A, ch 122, turn.
Row 1 Hdc into 3rd ch from hook, hdc into back loop of each ch across—120 sts. Turn.
Row 2 Hdc into back loops of first 12 sts, turn.
Row 3 Hdc into front loop of next 12 sts, turn.
Row 4 Hdc into back loops of next 11 sts, hdc2tog into back loops of next hdc of this row and next hdc of row 1, hdc into each st across, turn—119 sts.
Row 5 Hdc into front loop of first 12 sts, turn.
Row 6 Hdc into back loops of next 12 sts, turn.
Row 7 Hdc into front loop of next 11 sts, hdc2tog into front loop of next st of this row and next st of row 4, hdc into each st across—118 sts.
Row 8 Hdc into front loop of each st across. Fasten off.
Fold bag in half, lining up popcorn edging. Sew ends of strap into folded ends of bag. ▪

YARN

- 1¾oz/50g, 180yd/165m of any sport weight wool yarn in golden brown (A)
- 3½oz/100g, 200yd/183m of any worsted weight wool yarn in cranberry (B)

HOOKS

One each sizes F-5 and H-8 (3.75 and 5mm) crochet hooks
OR SIZE TO OBTAIN GAUGE

LEARN BY VIDEO
www.go-crafty.com

- ch
- Crocheting in the round
- dc
- hdc
- sc
- sl st

❯ SIZE

Sized for Adult Woman.

❯ MEASUREMENTS

Brim circumference 18"/45.5cm
Length 8½"/21.5cm

❯ GAUGE

4 (3 dc) clusters and 8 (dc and ch st) rnds to 3"/7.5cm over pat st using larger hook.
TAKE TIME TO CHECK YOUR GAUGE.

❯ NOTE

When changing colors, join yarn by sl st at end of rnd with the new color.

❯ HAT

With larger hook and A, ch 4, join with sl st to first ch to form ring.

Rnd 1 With A, ch 1, work 8 sc in ring. Join with sl st to first sc.

Rnd 2 With A, ch 1, work 2 sc in each sc—16 sc. Join with sl st to first sc.

Rnd 3 With A, ch 5, *skip next sc, 1 hdc in next sc, ch 3; rep from *, end sl st to 2nd ch of ch-5. There are 8 ch-3 spaces.

Rnd 4 With B, ch 1, then working over the ch-3 space and into the missed sc of previous rnd, *work 3 sc in missed sc, ch 1; rep from * end, join with sl st to first sc.

Rnd 5 With A, ch 1, sc back into the last ch-1 space of previous rnd, *ch 3, sc in next ch-1 space; rep from *, end ch 3, sl st to first sc to join.

Rnd 6 With A, ch 3, work 4 dc in first ch-3 space, then work 5 dc in each ch-3 space around, join to top of ch-3.

Rnd 7 With A, ch 1, sc back into last space, ch 6, *sc in next space after the 5 dc, ch 6; rep from * end, join to first sc.

Rnd 8 With B, ch 3, work 6 dc in first ch-6 space and 7 dc in each space around, join with sl st to top of ch-3.

Rnd 9 With A, ch 1, sc in same space, ch 5, *skip 4 dc, sc in next space after the 4 dc, ch 5; rep from *, end join to first sc—14 ch-5 spaces.

Rnd 10 With A, ch 3, work 5 dc in first ch-5 space and 6 dc in each space around, join—84 dc.

Rnd 11 With B, ch 1, sc back into last space, ch 7, *skip 6 dc, sc in next space after the 6 dc, ch 7; rep from * around, join to first sc.

Rnd 12 With A, ch 2 (does not count as 1 hdc), [work 9 hdc in each of next 5 ch-7 spaces, 10 hdc in next ch-7 space] twice, work 9 hdc in each of last 2 ch-7 spaces, join to top of first hdc—128 hdc.

Rnd 13 With B, ch 3 (counts as 1 dc), 1 dc in each of next 2 hdc, *skip 1 hdc, dc in each of next 3 hdc; rep from *, end join to top of ch-3.

Rnd 14 With A, ch 1, sc back into previous space, *ch 4, work 1 sc in between the next two 3-dc groups; rep from *, end join to first sc.

Rnd 15 With B, ch 3 (counts as 1 dc), 2 dc in first ch-4 space, *ch 1, 3 dc in next ch-4 space; rep from *, end ch 1, join to top of ch-3.

Rnd 16 With A, ch 1, sc back into previous space, *ch 4, 2 sc in next ch-1 space; rep from *, end ch 4, sc in same space as first sc, join to first sc.

Rnd 17 With B, ch 3, 3 dc in first ch space, then work 4 dc in each ch-sp around, join to top of ch-4.

Rnd 18 With A, ch 1, sc back into previous space, *ch 3, 1 sc in between the next two 4-dc groups; rep from *, end sl st to first sc.

Rnd 19 Rep rnd 17.

Rnd 20 Rep rnd 18.

Rnd 21 With B, ch 3, 2 dc in first space, then work 3 dc in each ch-sp around, join to top of ch-3.

Rnd 22 With A, ch 1, sc back into previous space, *ch 2, skip the 3 dc, 1 sc in between 2 sets of 3 dc; rep from *, end sl st to first sc.

Rnd 23 With B, ch 3, work 1 dc in first space, then work 2 dc in each ch space around, join to top of ch-3.
Change to smaller hook.

Rnd 24 With A, ch 2, work 1 hdc in each st around.

Rnd 25 Rep rnd 24.

Rnd 26 (WS) Turn work to the WS and with B, ch 2, work 1 hdc in each st around. Join and fasten off. ∎

color-tipped cowl >>>

YARN

5¼oz/150g, 342yd/312m of any
DK weight wool yarn each in teal (A)
and lime (B)

HOOK

Size 7 (4.5mm) crochet hook
OR SIZE TO OBTAIN GAUGE

LEARN BY VIDEO
www.go-crafty.com
- ch
- Crocheting in the round
- dc
- hdc
- sl st

) MEASUREMENTS

Circumference 28"/71cm
Length 12"/30.5cm

) GAUGE

Six 3-dc groups and 6 rnds to 4"/10cm over
pat st using size 7 (4.5mm) hook.
TAKE TIME TO CHECK YOUR GAUGE.

) COWL

With A, ch 114. Taking care not to twist ch,
join with sl st in first ch to form ring.
Rnd 1 Ch 2 (counts as first hdc), hdc in 2nd
ch from hook and in each ch around—114
hdc. Join with a sl st in top of beg ch.
Rnd 2 Rep rnd 1.

Beg pat stitch

Rnd 3 Ch 2, (counts as first dc), 2 dc in sp
between next 2 hdc, *sk 2 sp between hdc, 3
dc in next sp; rep from * around, join with a
sl st in top of beg ch.

Pat rnd Sc in next 2 dc, sc in sp between
3-dc grps, ch 2, 2 dc in same sp, *3 dc in next
sp between 3-dc grp; rep from * around, join
with sl st in top of beg ch.
Rep pat rnd for 16 rnds more. Fasten off.
Join B with a sl st in same sp between 3-dc
grps as join from previous rnd.
Next rnd Ch 2, 2 dc in same sp, *3 dc in next
sp between 3-dc grp; rep from * around, join
with sl st in top of beg ch.

With B, rep pat rnd for 17 rnds more. Rep
rnds 1 and 2.
Fasten off. ■

Jack Deutsch